Bernie Smithwick
and
THE SUPER RED BALL

William Coleman
Illustrated by Joan Artley Sterner

from David C. Cook Publishing Co.

I LOVE TO READ BOOKS encourage children to read—
all by themselves. Each Bible-based reader uses simple
vocabulary repeated over and over. Its lilting rhythm will
inspire your child to exclaim, "I love to read!" Soon the
child will read another book and another and another.
Before you know it, this love of books will last a lifetime!

Chariot Books is an imprint of David C. Cook Publishing Co.
David C. Cook Publishing Co., Elgin, Illinois 60120
David C. Cook Publishing Co., Weston, Ontario

BERNIE SMITHWICK AND THE SUPER RED BALL
© 1984 by William Coleman

Cover and illustrations by Joan Artley Sterner

First Printing, 1984
Printed in the United States of America

89 88 87 86 85 84   5 4 3 2 1

Library of Congress Cataloging in Publication Data
Coleman, William.
  Bernie Smithwick and the super red ball.
  (I love to read)
  Summary: Bernie's experiences with the super red
ball demonstrate the consequences of breaking rules
and disobeying one's parents.
  1. Children's stories, American. [1. Conduct of
life—Fiction] I. Sterner, Joan Artley, ill.
II. Title.
PZ7.C67725Bf   1984   [Fic.]   84-12172
ISBN 0-89191-822-1 (pbk.)

For Le and Loli Bouatic

Bernie Smithwick was a happy person.

He had curly hair and a wide smile.

Bernie was missing one tooth
right in the front.
And when he smiled,
you could see the space
where the tooth used to be.

Bernie liked to save things.
When he put his hand deep
into his pocket,
Bernie found lots of interesting
things.

If Bernie liked you
(and Bernie liked most people),
he would take a few things
out of his pocket
and show them to you.

Bernie might show you
his black rubber spider
with long legs
and white eyes.

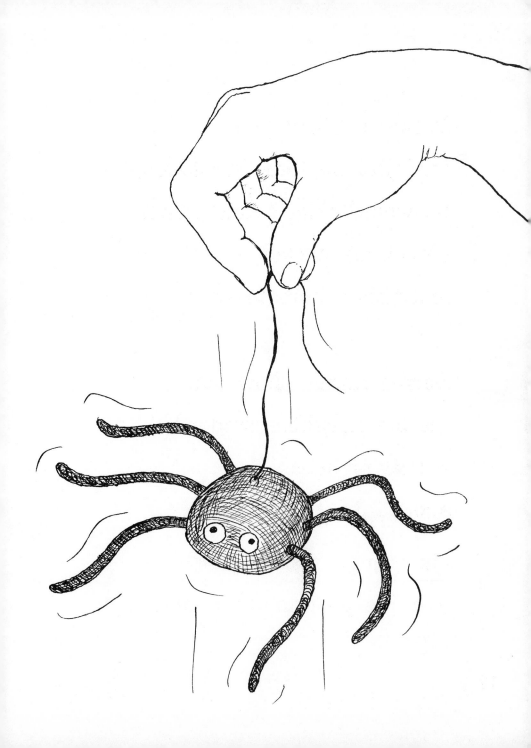

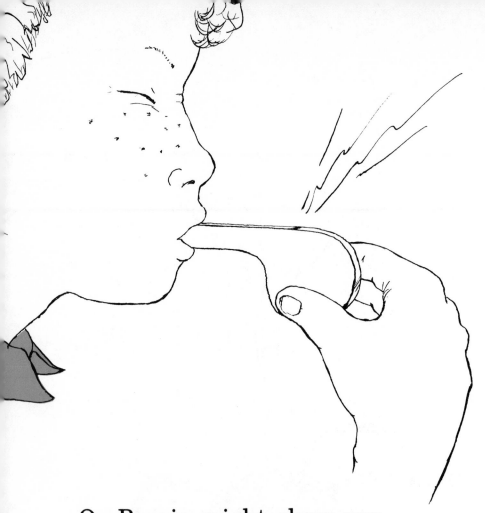

Or Bernie might show you
the orange whistle
that his grandmother gave him.

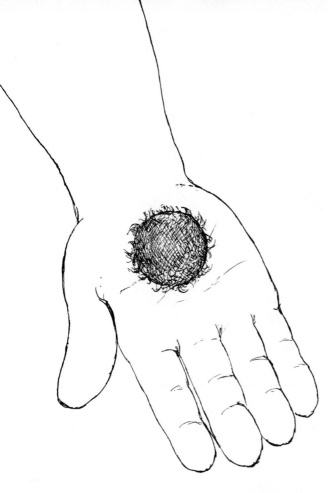

Next he might pull out
a dark purple candy ball
that was fuzzy
from being in his pocket.

If Bernie liked you a lot,
he might show you his
super red ball.

It was a special ball
with plenty of extra bounce.

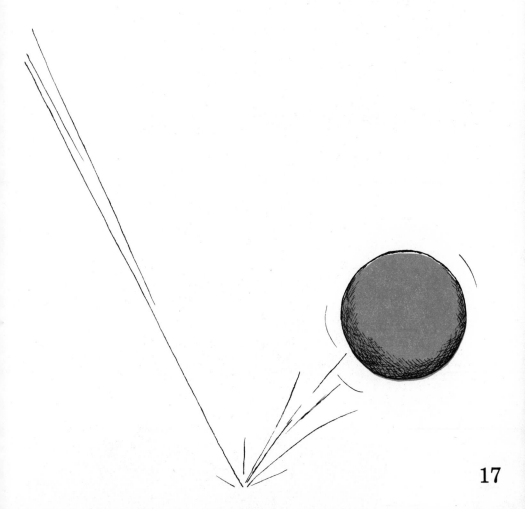

Bernie's super red ball
would bounce very high
when Bernie threw it hard
against the sidewalk.

19

Sometimes Bernie threw his

super red ball

against the side of the house.

21

It bounced back so fast
that it got lost.
And Bernie had to dig it out
from behind the garbage cans.

Bernie knew better,
but sometimes he
would throw the ball
at Roscoe, the cat.

And Roscoe didn't know
which way to run.

Bernie's mother told him,
"Never throw that ball
inside the house."
Bernie tried to remember,
but sometimes he forgot.

Most of the time
Bernie played with
his super red ball
without getting into trouble.

But on other days
he had trouble
keeping the ball
in his pocket
when he was in the house.

When his mother wasn't watching,
Bernie would bounce
the super red ball
against the ceiling.

When his mother wasn't watching,
Bernie would bounce the ball
against the wall.

When his mother wasn't watching,
Bernie would bounce
the super red ball
on the short table
in the living room.

When his mother wasn't watching,
Bernie would throw the ball
at Roscoe, the cat.

And Roscoe didn't know
what to do.

One day
Bernie threw his super red ball
too hard against the wood floor.

The ball bounced against the lamp
and knocked it down.

Next it bounced against
the picture of Uncle Fred
and knocked it down.

The super red ball bounced
against the fish bowl
and knocked it off the table
onto Roscoe's tail.

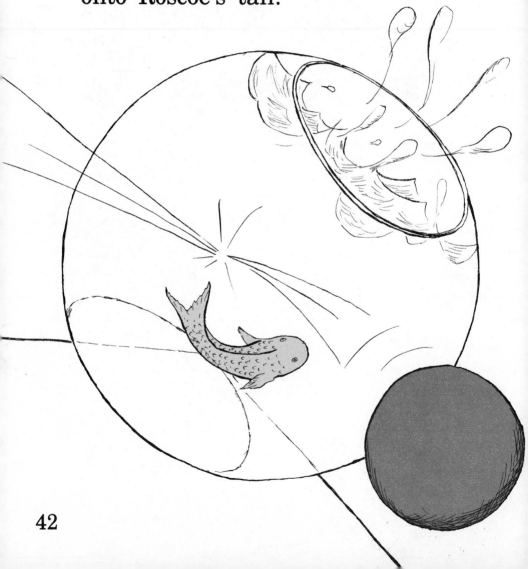

And Roscoe didn't know
what to do.

Bernie's mother ran into the room.
Bernie knew she would be mad.

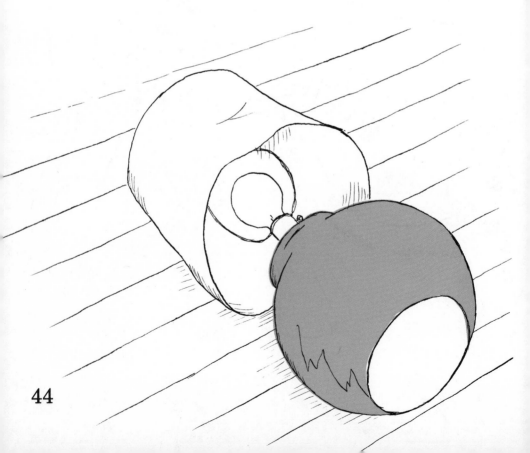

Bernie's mother said,
"I told you not to do that."
(That is what mothers
are supposed to say.)

Bernie felt bad.
He went to his room
and put a blanket
over his head.
You could just see
Bernie's eyes under
the blanket.

While Bernie was under
the blanket,
he got an idea.

Because he couldn't remember
to keep the super red ball
outside the house,
Bernie would tie
a long, yellow string
around his finger.
It would help him remember
to play with the super red ball
outside the house.

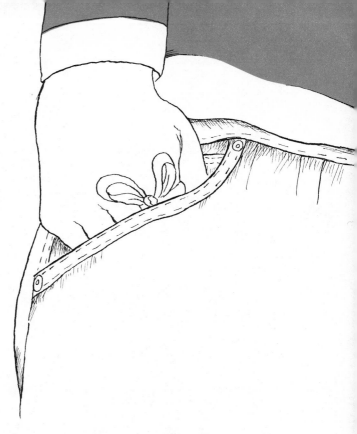

Every time Bernie
put his hand in his pocket
to take out his super red ball,
he felt the string on his finger.
Then he remembered not
to throw the super red ball
in the house.

Bernie felt good when he threw
the super red ball
outside the house.

He felt good
even when he had to
look for it behind
the garbage cans.

He still bounced the
super red ball
on the sidewalk.

He bounced the super red ball
off the house.

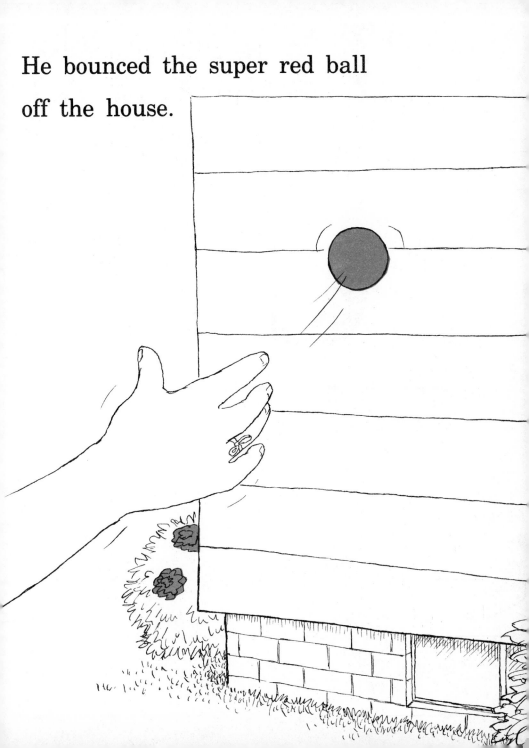

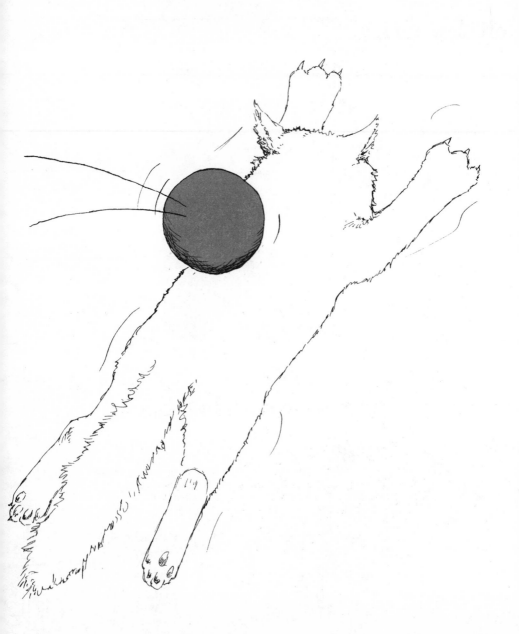

Bernie still threw
the super red ball
at Roscoe, the cat.

And Roscoe didn't know
what to do.

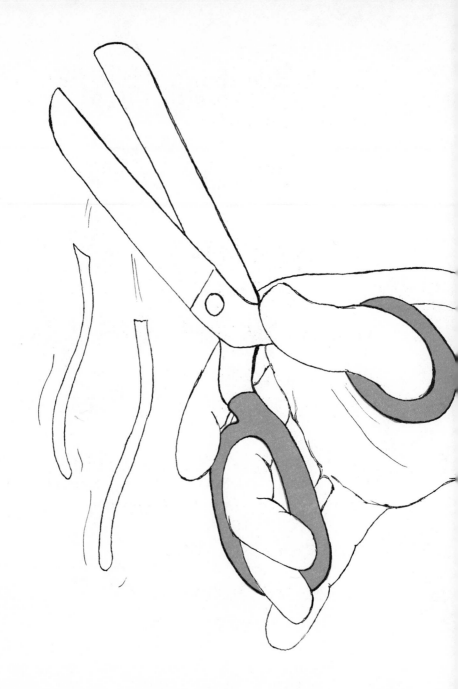

But Bernie didn't throw the
super red ball
inside the house anymore.

One day Bernie took a
large pair of scissors
and cut the string off
his finger.

Because now Bernie could
remember not to throw
the super red ball
inside the house.

Bernie was very happy.

Bernie's mother was very happy.

Bernie was learning to obey his parents.

And Roscoe didn't know
what to do.

"Young man, obey your father
and your mother.
Tie their instructions
around your finger
so you won't forget.
Take to heart all of their advice."

(Proverbs 6:20, 21, TLB)

Vocabulary

Of the 218 words used in this book, 196 are recommended by the Ginn Lexicon for grades one and two. The words recommended for grade three and above are starred.

a	fast	just	parents	tail
advice*	father		people	take
against	felt	keep	person	that
all	few	keeping	picture	the
an	finger	knew	play	their
and	fish	knocked	played	then
anymore*	floor	know	plenty*	things
are	for		pocket	threw
around	forget	lamp*	pull	throw
at	forgot	large	Proverbs*	tie
	found	learning	purple*	time
back	Fred	legs	put	to
bad	from	liked		told
ball	front	living	ran	too
be	fuzzy*	long	red	took
because		look	remember	tooth*
being	garbage*	lost	remembered	tried
behind	gave	lot	right	trouble
Bernie*	getting	lots	room	
better	good		Roscoe	uncle
black	got	mad	rubber*	under
blanket*	grandmother	man	run	used*
bounce		might		
bounced	had	missing	said	very
bowl	hair	most	save	
but	hand	mother	say	wall
	happy	mothers	scissors*	was
candy	hard		see	wasn't
cans	he	never	she	watching
cat	head	next	short	way
ceiling*	heart	not	show	went
could	help	now	side	what
couldn't*	high		sidewalk*	when
curly*	him	obey	smile	where
cut	his	of	smiled	which
	house	off	Smithwick*	while
dark		on	so	whistle
day	I	one	sometimes	white
days	idea	onto	space	wide
deep	if	or	special	with
didn't	in	orange	spider	without
dig	inside	other	still	wood
down	instructions*	out	string	won't
	interesting	outside	super*	would
even	into	over	supposed	
every	is			yellow
extra*	it	pair	table	you
eyes				young
				your